Texas
Plants and Animals

Mary Dodson Wade

Heinemann Library
Chicago, Illinois

a division of Reed Elsevier Inc.
Chicago, Illinois

Customer Service 888-454-2279

Visit our website at www.heinemannlibrary.com

Designed by Heinemann Library
Page layout by Patricia Stevenson
Printed and bound in the United States by
Lake Book Manufacturing, Inc.

08 07 06 05 04
10 9 8 7 6 5 4 3 2 1

Library of Congress Cataloging-in-Publication Data

Wade, Mary Dodson.
Texas plants and animals / Mary Dodson Wade.
p. cm. -- (Heinemann state studies)
Summary: Discusses the plants and animals and various ecosystems of
Texas including native and non-native species, as well as the impact of
humans on the environment and efforts at environmental and species
preservation and protection.
Includes bibliographical references (p.) and index.
ISBN 1-4034-0690-1 -- ISBN 1-4034-2698-8
1. Natural history--Texas--Juvenile literature. [1. Natural
history--Texas. 2. Endangered species.] I. Title. II. Series.
QH105.T4W29 2003
508.764--dc21

2003009562

Some words are shown in bold, **like this.** You can find out what they mean by looking in the glossary.

Acknowledgments

The author and publishers are grateful to the following for permission to reproduce copyright material:

Cover photographs by (main) David Muench/Corbis; (row, L-R) Martin B. Withers/Frank Lane Picture Agency/Corbis, Joe McDonald/Bruce Coleman Inc., David Muench/Corbis, Texas Parks and Wildlife Department

Title page (L-R) Joe McDonald/Corbis, David Muench/Corbis, William R. Curtsinger/National Geographic Images; contents page (L-R) Joe McDonald/Corbis, David Muench/Corbis; pp. 4, 12, 22T, 23B, 27B Joe McDonald/Corbis; p. 5 Rachel Epstein/The Image Works; pp. 6, 16T Texas Parks and Wildlife Department; p. 7 Karen Marks/Bat Conservation International; p. 8T D. Robert & Lorri Franz/Corbis; pp. 8B, 21B Darrell Gulin/Corbis; pp. 10, 11, 24, 25, 27T, 39 David Muench/Corbis; p. 14 William Ervin/Science Photo Library/Photo Researchers, Inc.; p. 15 Tom Brakefield/The Image Works; p. 16B Dale C. Spartas/Corbis; p. 17T Annie Griffiths Belt/Corbis; p. 17B Buddy Mays/Corbis; p. 18 David M. Schleser/Nature's Images, Inc./Photo Researchers, Inc.; p. 19 Frank Lane Picture Agency/Corbis; pp. 20T, 35 Tom Bean/Corbis; p. 20B Rick & Nora Bowers/Visuals Unlimited, Inc.; p. 21T Richard Cummins/Corbis; p. 22B Corbis; p. 23T Peter Johnson/Corbis; p. 26 Jack Dermio/Visuals Unlimited, Inc.; pp. 28, 32B Glen Mills/Texas Parks and Wildlife Department; p. 30 Jack Lewis/Texas Department of Transportation; p. 31T Joe Tucciarone/Science Photo Library/Photo Researchers, Inc.; p. 31B Scott Berner/Visuals Unlimited, Inc.; p. 32T A. J. Copley/Visuals Unlimited, Inc.; p. 33 Quetzalcoatlus Northropi/From the Collections of the Texas Memorial Museum; p. 34 Gianni Dagli Orti/Corbis; p. 36 W. Perry Conway/Corbis; p. 37 William R. Curtsinger/National Geographic Images; p. 38T Joe McDonald/Visuals Unlimited, Inc.; p. 38B Kevin Schafer/Corbis; p. 41 Larry J. Borks/Tyler Rose Festival; p. 42 Ralph Lauer/AP Wide World Photos; p. 43 Glenn Longley; p. 44 Bob Daemmrich/The Image Works

Photo research by Dawn Friedman

Special thanks to John Herron, Branch Chief, Wildlife Diversity, of the Texas Parks and Wildlife Department, for his comments in the preparation of this book.

Every effort has been made to contact copyright holders of any material reproduced in this book. Any omissions will be rectified in subsequent printings if notice is given to the publisher.

Contents

Introduction

As the second-largest state, it is no wonder that Texas has a great variety of plants and animals. Raccoons wander among the pine trees of eastern Texas. Alligators live in the coastal **marshes** and swamps. Quail fly out of High Plains grasses. Javelinas root through the southern **brush.** White-tailed deer cover the hill country. Prairie dogs dig tunnels beneath the prairies of western Texas.

There are over 140 **species** of land mammals **native** to Texas, and several types of marine mammals, such as dolphins, offshore. About 100 species of snakes live throughout the state of Texas. More than 540 species of birds either live in Texas or **migrate** across it each year. Monarch butterflies also migrate across the state in large numbers.

*Roadrunners live in dry grasslands and **semi-desert habitats** in Texas. Though these birds are able to fly, they prefer to run—at speeds up to seventeen miles per hour!*

Saving Texas Longhorns

Will C. Barnes of the Texas Forest Service saved Texas longhorns from **extinction.** Very few were left in 1927, when Barnes and fellow foresters collected a small herd in southern Texas. They took the longhorns to the Wichita Mountains National Wildlife Refuge in Oklahoma.

J. Frank Dobie and Sid Richardson put longhorns into state parks in the 1930s. The herds have since increased enough for extra cattle to be sold.

Longhorn

Texas chose the longhorn as its state large mammal. The longhorn cattle in the state today **descend** from cattle that escaped from early Spanish herds. They mixed with English cattle brought to Texas in the 1820s. Longhorns, which are not as fat as English cattle, had fewer diseases and thrived on poor-quality grass.

The name of the cattle came from their enormous horns, which can be eight feet wide from tip to tip. While the horns can be straight, most have gentle or sharp curves in them.

Before the Civil War, more than 10 million wild longhorns lived in the United States. By 1927, fewer than 30 Texas longhorns were left. People now breed longhorns to increase their numbers.

ARMADILLO

The armadillo is the official Texas state small mammal. The Spanish named this bony-plated creature *armadillo,* which means "little armored thing." Armadillos are native to South America. Armadillos do not do well in dry areas or extreme cold. They are not found in far western Texas.

An armadillo is about the size of a large cat. Each litter consists of four identical young. Armadillos jump three or four feet off the ground if startled. They can run as fast as a squirrel. To cross a body of water, armadillos sometimes hold their breath and walk across the bottom. Many people consider them pests because they dig up lawns, looking for grubs and insects. Armadillos have few natural **predators,** but they cannot see or hear well and often get run over by cars and trucks.

Nine-banded armadillos arrived in the Rio Grande Valley in the mid-1850s.

Bats in the City

The world's largest known colony of **urban** bats is in Austin, Texas. One and a half million Mexican free-tailed bats live under the Congress Avenue Bridge. At one point, people in Austin were asking to have the bats removed. Now, however, they are a big tourist attraction. The bats come out each evening and eat thousands of pounds of mosquitoes during the night.

Bats

Mexican, or Brazilian, free-tailed bats are the Texas state flying mammal. Bats fly at night to catch insects, especially mosquitoes. Texas has more **species** of bats than any other state. Most of the bats in Texas are Mexican free-tailed bats. Bracken Cave, in south-central Texas, has the world's largest group of bats—over twenty million. Public viewing is limited to protect the bats. People watch millions of bats come out at the Eckert James River Bat Cave Preserve, southwest of Mason, and at Frio Bat Cave, near Concan. Two abandoned railroad tunnels—Old Tunnel Wildlife Management Area, near Fredericksburg, and the Clarity Tunnel in Caprock Canyons Trailway State Park, about 100 miles southeast of Amarillo—also have large bat colonies.

Mockingbirds get their name from their ability to copy sounds they hear.

Mockingbird

Mockingbirds live in almost every type of habitat in the state of Texas. Most live in the state all year, but some migrate south to Mexico. The mockingbird is known for fiercely defending its territory. It has over 2,000 different calls, many of which are sounds it copies from other birds. Their diet includes fruits, vegetables, and insects.

Prickly Pear Cactus

The prickly pear cactus blooms with yellow or orange flowers. In rare cases, the flowers are almost red. Species can have purple leaves or fruit. Some prickly pear found in Texas can grow six or seven feet high. The prickly pear cactus became the state plant in 1995.

Bluebonnet

Since 1901, bluebonnet has been the state flower of Texas. Six species of the flower grow in the state. In west Texas, Big Bend bluebonnet grows up to three feet tall. Most of central Texas is covered with another variety of bluebonnet, which has deeper blue blossoms.

Brightly colored Texas bluebonnets attract a large variety of moths and butterflies.

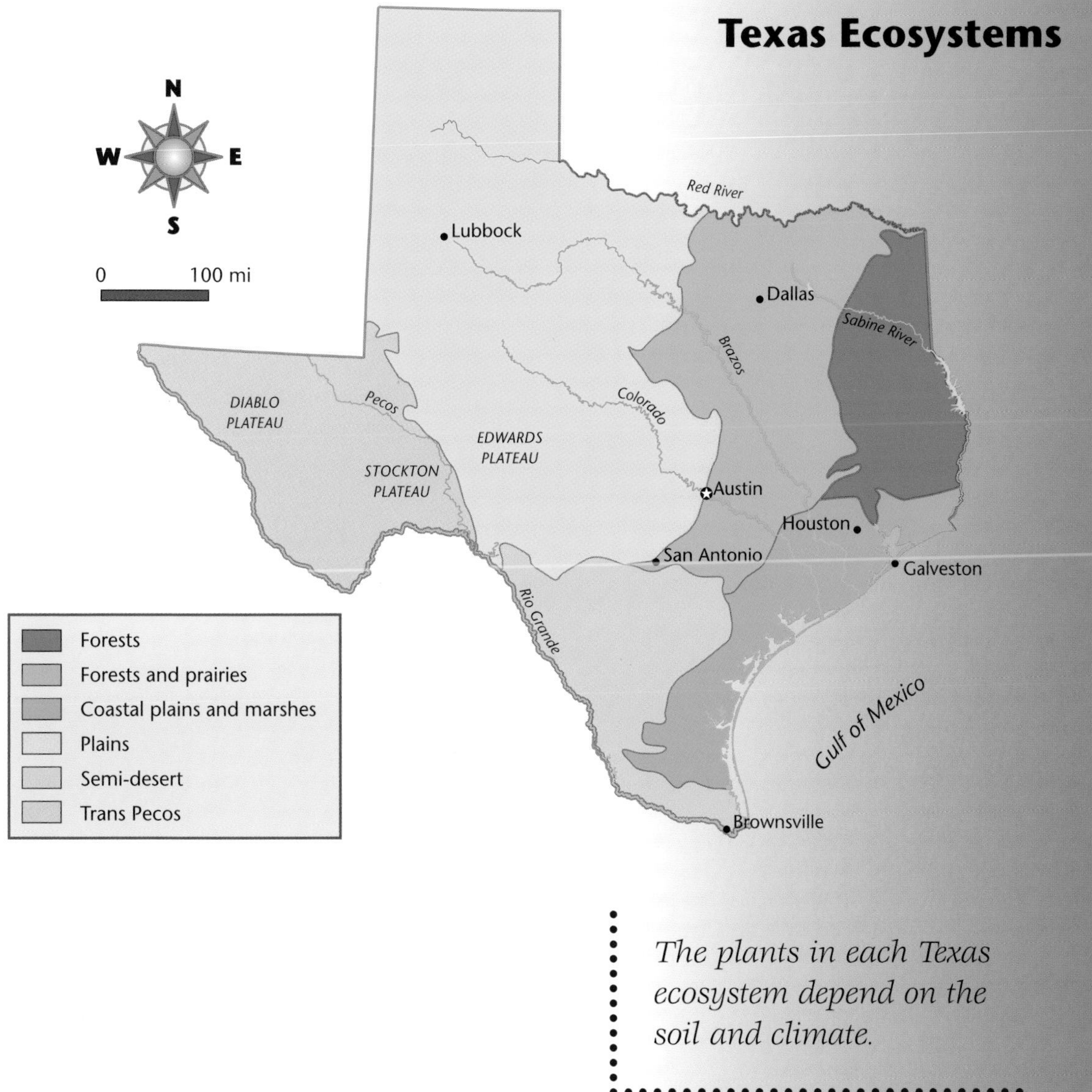

The plants in each Texas ecosystem depend on the soil and climate.

Many Habitats

The state of Texas includes multiple **ecosystems** full of many different plants and animals. The prairies, forests, plateaus, plains, **semi-desert** regions, and coastal marshes all have unique offerings of their own. Together, all that they offer adds up to the great variety of species found within the state, with some species living in multiple habitats.

Forests

Texas forests make up one of several **ecosystems** in the state. Forests cover about 22 million acres in the state—an area larger than Massachusetts, Connecticut, New Hampshire, and Vermont combined. Almost all of Texas's forested lands, or woodlands, are in eastern Texas, which has a mild **climate.** Eastern Texas has numerous rivers and streams and enough rainfall to grow healthy grasses and trees. All four of Texas's national forests and all five state forests are in eastern Texas.

The Big Thicket National Preserve includes a large pine and hardwood forest.

Plants of the Forest

Half of the trees in the forests of Texas are pines. Native varieties

Thick groves of longleaf pine trees grow in the East Pine Woods.

include loblolly, shortleaf, and longleaf pines. After pines, oak and hickory trees are the most numerous. Together, pine, oak, and hickory make up about 90% of the forest trees. Hardwoods such as willow, maple, sweetgum, and cottonwood also grow in Texas forests.

The forest floor is often covered with blackseed needlegrass, wildrye, woodoats, purpletop, and bluestem grasses. Other shrubs and vines found in Texas forests include trumpet honeysuckle, dogwood, redbud, and poison ivy.

The copperhead snakes in Texas blend in well with the leaves on forest floors.

Animals of the Forest

Many **species** of animals make their home in Texas's forests. Squirrels, foxes, skunks, and raccoons live in the forest. Opossums have been in Texas since the time of the last dinosaurs. Poisonous snakes in this area include copperheads, coral snakes, and cottonmouths. Other wildlife such as anole lizards, praying mantis, lacewings, and ladybugs flourish in the mild **climate** of the forest.

Texas Forest Food Web

There are many food chains in the forest **habitats** of Texas. A **food chain** shows how different plants and animals in a habitat rely on one another for food. One species becomes food for another. The overlapping system of multiple food chains within an **ecosystem** is called a **food web.**

One example of a Texas forest food web is shown here. Plants in the forest are eaten by ants and white-tailed deer. The ants, in turn, may be eaten by blue jays and opossums. A bobcat may then eat the deer, bird, or opossum.

Birds such as blue jays and mockingbirds are common in the eastern half of Texas. Pine warblers, wood ducks, pileated woodpeckers, brown-headed nuthatches, and **endangered** red-cockaded woodpeckers also appear in the forests of eastern Texas.

The Coast

Salt and freshwater **marshes** occur all along the 625 miles of Texas Gulf Coast. The Gulf Marshes are on a narrow strip of lowlands along the coast and on the barrier islands just off the coast. These marshes are the natural **habitat** for a wide variety of water birds and other wildlife.

National Wildlife Refuges

Texas Point National Wildlife **Refuge** (NWR), near the Texas-Louisiana border, is on the **migration** route for peregrine falcons and **endangered** southern bald eagles. Seaside sparrows live only in a tiny area of salt marshes near Sabine Pass. Besides birds, McFaddin NWR, near Beaumont, is also home to a large population of alligators. High Island's live oak trees provide a place for exhausted migrating warblers to rest. Brazoria NWR, in Freeport, has roseate spoonbills, great blue herons,

The anhinga is a coastal bird found in Texas. It spears fish under the water with its sharp bill, then takes its food back to land to eat. Many water birds use this method of hunting.

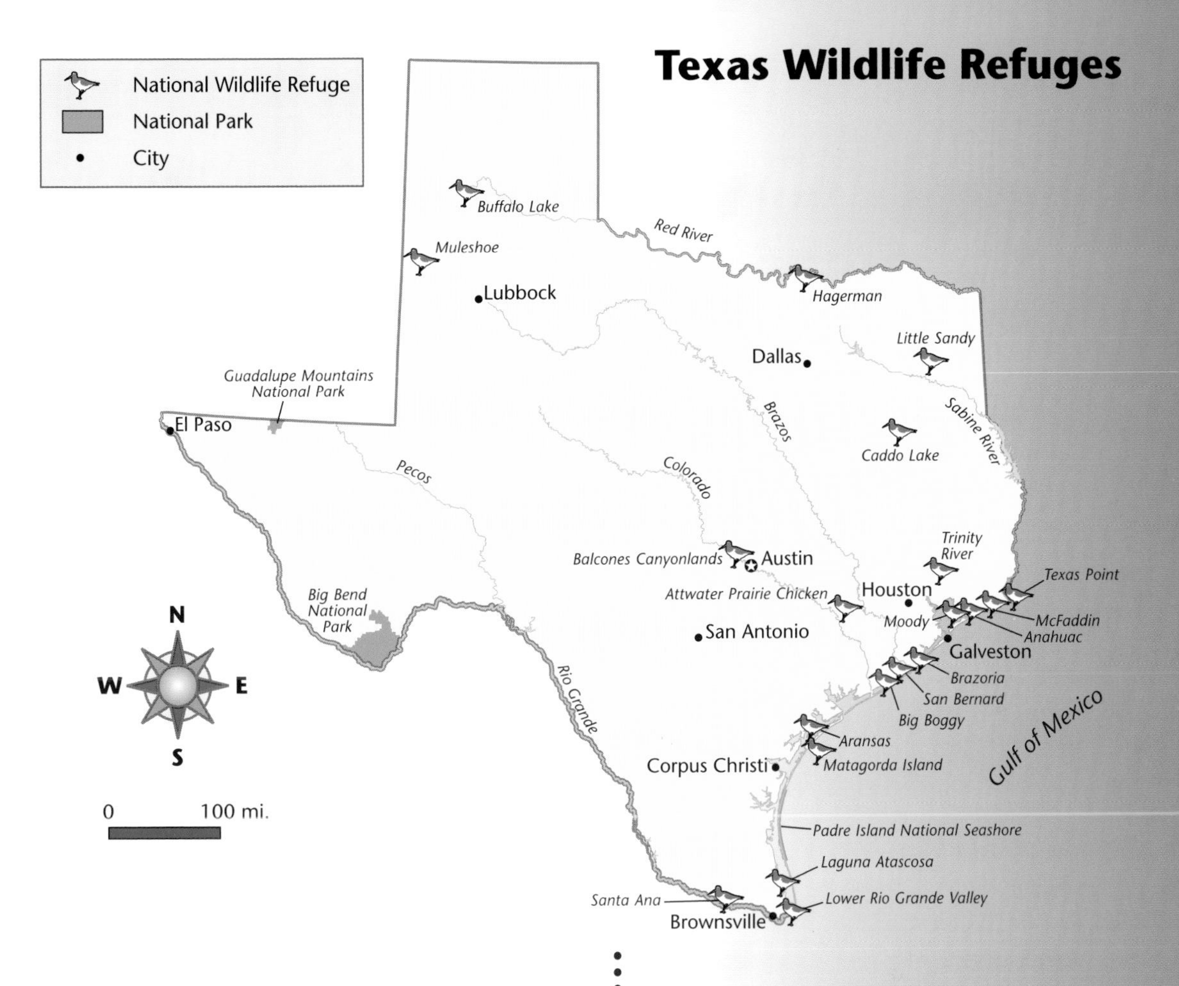

white ibis, sandhill cranes, peregrine falcons, reddish egrets, and scissor-tailed flycatchers.

About half of the state's national wildlife refuges are along the coast.

Aransas NWR, winter home of whooping cranes, has the largest number of bird **species** of any refuge in the country. Laguna Atascosa NWR, on the lower Rio Grande, has the largest winter **concentration** of red-headed ducks in the United States. The lower Rio Grande Valley is the only place in the United States to find green jays and chachalacas.

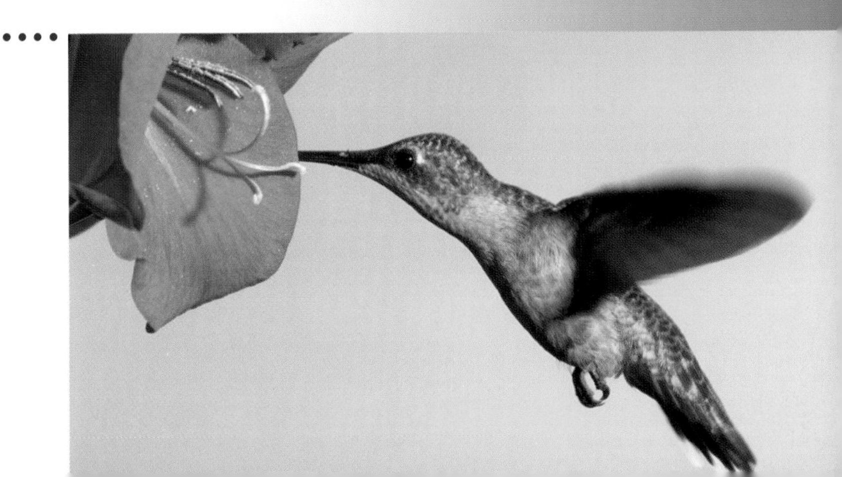

Thousands of ruby-throated hummingbirds ***migrate*** *through the Aransas NWR. The hummingbird's wings beat so quickly, they are just a blur in this photograph.*

The lightning whelk is the official state shell of Texas. This mollusk has a long shell with brown stripes.

Water Life

The variety of animals found on land in Texas is equaled or exceeded by the variety of animals found in the surrounding waters. Salt **marshes** are home to blue crabs, stone crabs, hermit crabs, mud crabs, and fiddler crabs. You can also find oysters, mussels, and eels in a Texas salt marsh.

Coastal bays are the **habitat** of more fish, including Southern flounder, red drum, black drum, and Atlantic croaker. The off-shore waters of the Gulf of Mexico are home to coral, sponges, kingfish, shrimp, and bottle-nosed dolphins. Lightning whelk live in the Gulf Coast sands.

Coastal Plants

Plants in the Gulf Marshes include rushes, cordgrasses, seashore saltgrass, common reeds, sedges, and seashore dropseed. Southern magnolias thrive in Texas's warm coastal **climate.** Cypress trees grow in freshwater swamps along the coast and in eastern Texas lakes.

Red drum, or redfish, live in shallow waters along the coast of the Gulf of Mexico.

Swaying in the Wind

Palm trees thrive in a warm, humid coastal **climate.** New branches called fronds grow from the center of the plant, and the outer fronds are attached with crisscrossing fibers that reach around the tree. Because the trunk is not rigid, the trees bend without breaking during hurricanes. In this photo of Corpus Christi during Hurricane Allen in 1980, the palm trees are swaying in the strong winds.

One of the oldest known coastal live oaks is in Goose Island State Park, near Rockport. This tree is estimated to be 1,000 years old. Live oaks get their name because their limbs are never bare. They lose their leaves around February, but other leaves are already growing in at that point, ready to take their place.

One of the oldest live oaks is near Rockport, Texas.

Plains, Prairies, and Plateaus

Much of Texas is made up of prairies, plains, and plateaus. Prairies and plains stretch across the lowlands, while plateaus and high plains cover the uplands. The 100th **meridian** is a **longitude** line that runs through Texas. American settlers moving westward across the state learned that there was too little rain west of the meridian to raise many crops.

Prairies

About 150 miles east of the 100th **meridian,** the cities of Dallas and Fort Worth sit, about 30 miles apart. They

Sideoats gramma, the state grass of Texas, grows on the prairies. About 570 different varieties of grasses grow in Texas—more than in any other state.

Bison

American bison once freely roamed the Texas plains. Sixty million bison grazed as far south as the Concho River, near San Angelo. Bison provided everything that Plains Indians needed. As a way to make sure that Native Americans stayed on the reservations in Oklahoma, the U.S. government killed the bison. Ranchers Charles Goodnight and Charles J. "Buffalo" Jones saved small herds, and that kept them from becoming extinct. Some bison in Texas are now on private ranches, but they are mostly in zoos. One of the last wild herds of bison lives on the Texas plains.

are both on prairies, but the land west of Fort Worth, called the Cross Timber Prairie, is very different from the land to the east. Dallas is in the Blackland Prairie, a part of the tallgrass prairie. Originally both prairies were covered with little and big bluestem, switchgrass, buffalo grass, and sideoats gramma. Rich soil on the Blackland Prairie, however, made it valuable farmland. The prairie was slowly converted for agricultural use. Only about one percent of true Blackland Prairie remains today.

Javelinas, or collared peccaries, look a little like wild boars, but they are a different ***species.***

EDWARDS PLATEAU

In the rocky soil of the Edwards Plateau, in central Texas, shinnery oaks and cedars share the land with sheep, goats, and the largest **concentration** of white-tailed deer in the United States. Cypress trees grow along the streams. Pecan, juniper, and live oak trees grow in places with enough moisture. Plateau grasses include bluestem, indiangrass, switchgrass, sideoats gramma, and buffalograss.

Rugged canyons on the upper Sabinal River **watershed** provide shelter for rare green kingfishers and the **endangered** black-capped vireo. Golden-cheeked warblers nest in Lost Maples State Park during the summer. South Llano River State Park, in Kimble County, has wooded **bottomland** where Rio Grande turkeys spend the winter. Wood ducks, javelinas, foxes, beavers, bobcats, and armadillos are also found in the area.

The number of black-capped vireos is closely monitored in Edwards Plateau and in various Texas counties.

Lady Bird Johnson Wildflower Center

Lady Bird Johnson Wildflower Center in Austin is the only **conservation** center in the nation that limits itself to native plants of North America. The center is named for the wife of President Lyndon Baines Johnson. While she was first lady, she began a nationwide project of using native plants to beautify the country. The Wildflower Center emphasizes using **xeriscape** for decorative plants. These native plants use less water than regular garden flowers.

Wildflowers

About 5,000 varieties of wildflowers grow in Texas. The variety depends on the soil and rainfall. The Edwards Plateau is particularly known for wildflowers. Since 1930, the Texas Department of Transportation (TxDOT) has planted wildflowers along highways. The plants keep soil from **eroding** as they display a sea of colors. Bluebonnets, orange Indian paintbrush, pink or yellow primroses, lavender verbenas, purple phlox, and red clover are a bright, colorful sight for motorists. The wildflowers grow again each year by themselves, but TxDOT also plants more each year to keep them in large supply.

Bluebonnets color the landscape along a Texas highway.

Desert cottontails sometimes live in burrows that have been left behind by other animals, such as prairie dogs.

High Plains

The Panhandle is a flat, dry region that was once a short-grass prairie. Today, the High Plains north of Hale County is part of the great "Breadbasket" of America. Fields on the plains grow wheat and grain sorghum. Prairie dogs, white-tailed deer, quail, flickers, and horned larks are found throughout the dry areas of western Texas.

Prairie Dog Towns

Prairie dogs are similar to ground squirrels. They got their name because they make a yip or barking sound similar to that of a small dog. They live in underground burrows in large colonies called towns. There are prairie dog towns in parks in Lubbock, Big Spring, and Snyder.

Flocks of snow geese can often be seen flying over lakes in the High Plains.

The High Plains are on the Central Flyway for **migrating** birds. **Playas** there form lakes when it rains and attract the birds. In winter, Muleshoe NWR's three playas have the largest **concentration** of sandhill cranes in the country. Buffalo Lake NWR in Randall County provides 7,000 acres of **wetlands** for birds—including northern bobwhites, horned larks, western meadowlarks, redwing blackbirds, great blue herons, hawks, ducks, and geese. The **refuge** also has some of the nation's best shortgrass prairie. Buffalo Lake is kept wet to provide a home for the numerous birds, reptiles, and **mammals.**

Great blue herons eat fish, frogs, turtles, snakes, and lizards. They often use their sharp beak to spear their food.

Mesquite and cacti grow in Santa Ana National Wildlife Refuge.

Mesquite and cactus cover much of the drier parts of Texas. Mesquite is a small tree with feathery leaves and long thorns. Growing in the sands in the area are sand sagebrush, buffalograss, prickly pear, blue gramma, and yucca. Scorpions, tarantulas, and rattlesnakes live there, too.

Canyons cut through the High Plains region. Cottonwood trees and plum **thickets** grow where there is moisture at the bottom. Bobcats, porcupines, and foxes make their home in the canyons, as well as quail, mourning doves, mule deer, wild turkeys, and auodad sheep.

Semi-Desert Regions

Southern Texas is hot and dry. The land is filled with **brush.** Acacia, huisache, agurita, creosote, cholla, and palo verde grow in very dry conditions. These plants store water. The thick, spiked leaves of the agave produce aloe, a substance used in hand lotion and to help heal minor burns. The common name for agave is century plant, but the plants do not actually live 100 years. A mature plant will eventually send up a single tall spike with a blossom on top. Soon afterward, the plant dies. Coyotes, javelinas, ocelots, and jaguarundis live in the brush country.

This century plant grows near the Chisos Mountains in Big Bend National Park.

*The Texas palmetto is **native** to the far south of Texas and can survive in very high desert temperatures.*

The Valley

The area near the mouth of the Rio Grande is called the Valley. The area is known for citrus crops and the palm trees of many varieties that grow there. The sabal palm is **endangered.** The biggest group of this palm with fan-shaped fronds is in the Sabal Palm Grove Wildlife **Sanctuary,** near Brownsville.

Trans Pecos

The area west of the Pecos River is called Trans Pecos. The highest peaks in the state are here, but other parts are flat, desertlike areas. The variation in **altitude** gives this part of Texas different kinds of animals than the well-watered eastern half of the state.

Within Guadalupe Peak National Park, there are four **ecosystems:** forest, meadow, canyon, and desert. At 7,000 feet, ponderosa pines and aspens shade wapiti grazing in an alpine meadow. The wapiti were brought in from North Dakota when **native** elk became **extinct.** A grassy meadow at 5,000 feet has pine and hardwood trees. Raccoons, porcupines, and mule deer make their home in McKittrick Canyon. Trees in the canyon are known for their beautiful fall colors. The desert below, at 3,000 feet, provides a **habitat** for prickly pear cacti, kangaroo rats, and coyotes.

Some of the plants in the Trans-Pecos area are not found anywhere else in the state. These include mountain muhly and Arizona fescue. Poisonous plants in the area include threadleaf groundsel, broom snakeweed, rayless goldenrod, twoleaf senna, and loco.

Most varieties of cactus will thrive in a dry **climate.** Prickly pear is the most common of Texas's 100 varieties of cactus. The thick, spine-covered pads, or leaves, hold water. During dry times, ranchers burn off the spines and feed the pads to livestock.

Cacti can be found throughout the ***semi-desert*** *regions of Texas.*

The Texas madrone, a small tree with red wood, grows in upland areas of Trans Pecos. Cottonwoods grow along streams. Pronghorns live in open grassy areas. Texas bighorn sheep were once **extirpated** from the state. Now that they have been **reintroduced,** they have to compete with nonnative Barbary sheep, or aoudad, for land and food. Diamondback rattlesnakes are plentiful. The Mojave rattlesnake has the most deadly venom of any snake in North America.

Mojave rattlesnakes live only in the westernmost parts of the state.

Big Bend National Park was the first national park in Texas. It is the size of Rhode Island. The Chisos Mountains are entirely within its boundaries. **Elevations** range from sea level along the Rio Grande to 7,000-foot-high peaks. The park has 1,100 **species** of plants, 78 species of **mammals,** 56 species of reptiles, and 35 species of fish. It has more kinds of birds than any other park in the country, with 434 species.

Endangered black-capped vireos, and Mexican long-nosed bats are found here. Only in the park can you find the Big Bend gambusia, Del Carmen white-tailed deer, and Mexican drooping juniper. Animals such as peregrine falcons, coyotes, javelinas, gray foxes, skunks, raccoons, and jackrabbits also live in the park. Occasionally, black bears and mountain lions may be spotted in the area.

About 100 to 150 Colima warblers live in the Chisos Mountains—their only nesting site in the United States. The bird can be recognized by the bright yellow feathers on the underside of its long, gray tail.

Texas of Yesterday

Millions of years ago, the **climate** and landscape of Texas were different than they are today. So were the plants and animals. When an animal's **habitat** is destroyed, the **species** may become **extinct.**

Like many other parts of the world, Texas contains evidence of the creatures that lived there many thousands, even millions, of years ago. Scientists have found **fossils** of Texas plants and animals from long ago. These fossils help us learn more about the state's natural history.

Dinosaurs in Texas

The dinosaur age happened during a **geological** time called the Mesozoic **Era.** This era is divided into three periods. Texas had dinosaurs during the first period, called the Triassic. It also had dinosaurs in both parts of the last period, the Early and Late Cretaceous.

Texas had theropods and sauropods, armored dinosaurs, and even flying reptiles. Theropods were meat-eating

Mesozoic Era—The Age of Dinosaurs

Triassic 245 million to 208 million years ago

Jurassic 208 million to 144 million years ago

Cretaceous 144 million to 66 million years ago

- *Early Cretaceous* 144 million to 97.5 million years ago
- *Late Cretaceous* 97.5 to 66 million years ago

The Houston Museum of Natural History has a Diplodocus skeleton on display. Fossil footprints of the late-Jurassic dinosaur were found in Texas in the 1930s.

dinosaurs that walked on their hind legs. Sauropods were plant-eating dinosaurs that walked on all four legs. No place on Earth, including Texas, had all 300 **species** of known dinosaurs.

With the exception of eastern Texas, dinosaur remains have been found in every part of the state. Three places—the Panhandle, central Texas, and the Big Bend—had large groups of dinosaurs that lived during different time periods.

Triassic

Triassic dinosaurs lived 220 million years ago in what is now Texas. At that time, North America was still part of the huge **supercontinent** we call Pangaea. As few as two or as many as seven species of dinosaurs may have lived in Texas during the Triassic period. Theropods were found in the Texas Panhandle, near Lubbock, Post, and Big Spring. Plant-eaters were found near Post.

Early Cretaceous

Cretaceous dinosaurs lived 114 million years ago in what is now central Texas. By that time, North America had

Tenontosaurus lived in Texas swamps during the Early Cretaceous period.

broken away from the other continents and was beginning to take the shape it has today. During this time, eastern and southern Texas were under water. At least ten species of Early Cretaceous dinosaurs lived in Texas. Most of them were within 100 miles of Dallas and Fort Worth.

Dinosaur Valley State Park

Tracks left in soft mud that turned to stone millions of years ago were found in the Paluxy River near Glen Rose. One set of fossil footprints seems to show an Acrocanthosaurus, a three-toed meat-eating dinosaur, running alongside a plant-eating dinosaur called Pleurocoelus. The Pleurocoelus tracks are 24 to 36 inches across. They were the first tracks of a plant-eating dinosaur ever discovered. Some of the tracks were dug up from the ground in the 1940s and taken to the American Museum of Natural History in New York City. Pleurocoelus is the official Texas state dinosaur.

A fossil of a Plesiosaurus, a water reptile from the Late Cretaceous period, was discovered in Texas while the Dallas-Fort Worth airport was being built.

Late Cretaceous

Dinosaurs of the Late Cretaceous period lived 97.5 million to 66 million years ago. Layers of rock from this period contain an amazing number of different **fossils.**

Two different layers of rocks in the Big Bend area contain Late Cretaceous dinosaurs. One layer has horned dinosaurs called Chasmosaurus and Torosaurus, as well as the duckbilled Hadrosaurus. A jawbone assumed to be from a Tyrannosaurus rex was also found. Another layer contained the huge sauropod called Alamosaurus. This puzzled scientists because they thought there had been no sauropods in North America for 35 million years. Scientists supposed the Alamosaurus could only have entered Texas from South America.

At the end of the Late Cretaceous period, dinosaurs everywhere suddenly died out. Nobody knows exactly why.

*A **prehistoric** plant called palmwood is the Texas state stone. The palmwood shown here is petrified—it turned to stone through a natural process.*

Big Texas Dinos

Alamosaurus does not get its name from the famous Texas Alamo. *Alamo* is the Spanish word for cottonwood tree. The Alamosaurus dinosaur was first discovered at a Navajo trading post in New Mexico called Alamo, which is how it got the name. Alamosaurus was the largest of the Big Bend dinosaurs. Another creature, a **bivalve,** measured three feet wide and four feet long. A giant crocodile had a six-foot-long skull. Even more remarkable was the flying dinosaur Quetzalcoatlus (above), which scientists named after the feathered serpent god of the Aztecs. With a wingspan of almost 40 feet, Quetzalcoatlus was the largest animal ever to fly.

Prehistoric Texas

After the age of the dinosaurs, the age of **mammals** began. The **climate** changed. Early horses, camels, sloths, giant armadillos, bats, rats, and big cats developed. Plants such as palmwood grew.

The climate in Texas warmed and cooled as the **glaciers** covering the northern half of North America melted and reformed. From 30,000 to 22,500 B.C.E., the climate was stable. Grasses filled the area north and west of Austin. Oak and hickory forests extended through eastern Texas. Pine, juniper, Douglas fir, and spruce trees grew in the higher **elevations** of the Guadalupe and Chisos Mountains of western Texas.

During the **ice age** that occurred between 22,500 and 8,000 B.C.E., the **climate** was much cooler. Giant bison, horses, and camels lived in Texas. There were also some

Ice Age mammoths died out in Texas as the climate became warmer and drier.

relatives of today's elephants—mastodons and mammoths. Forests grew lower on the mountain slopes. The Panhandle developed **playas**—round lakes that catch rainwater. Forests in eastern Texas had pine, oak, elm, spruce, maple, hazelnut, alder, and birch trees.

About 10,000 B.C.E., the **glaciers** melted. Warm winds blowing high above the earth moved northward. Playas dried up. Forests of pine, Douglas fir, and juniper spread upwards toward mountain peaks in Texas. Spruce trees disappeared. Grasslands stretched from what is today San Angelo to El Paso. In the Lower Pecos River area, piñon pines and junipers grew only in canyons and protected hills. Desert plants such as cactus, agave, and yucca moved into southern Texas. Some areas became **semi-desert** regions. In the Edwards Plateau, oak and juniper became plentiful. In eastern Texas, most older trees disappeared and loblolly pines became plentiful. New **species** of oak, hickory, walnut, pecan, sweet gum, and elm trees developed. North-central Texas turned into a grassy **savanna.** By 8000 B.C.E., the landscape was much as it is today.

A brief cooling period occurred about 2,500 years ago. Cool conditions reached all the way to the Rio Grande. Large herds of bison grazed near Langtry and Del Rio. Then the landscape we know today developed.

Endangered Species

As settlers moved to Texas throughout the 1800s and 1900s, cities grew, causing many wildlife **habitats** to disappear. Some of the plants and animals that lived in these habitats became **extinct.** Many became **endangered.** Some became **threatened,** which means that the numbers are dropping and there is cause for concern. The species may become endangered in the near future.

Today, many of Texas's endangered animals can be found in the 122 state parks and five state forests. National parks, forests, and seashores protect wildlife as well. Losing one species in an **ecosystem** can lead to the loss of other species as well. For that reason, people have to work together to protect all living things.

Whooping Crane

Among the most visible of the endangered Texas animals is the whooping crane. Adult whooping cranes are the tallest birds in the United States. They stand five feet tall on their slender legs. Their wingspan is seven and a half feet.

Whooping cranes feed on clams, snails, frogs, mice, berries, acorns, and fish.

Whooping crane pairs mate for life. Each family usually consists of the two adults and one young bird. The family claims one square mile of coastal **territory.** The mates return to the same spot each year. They defend their territory with their long, tough beaks.

Attwater's Prairie Chicken

Attwater's prairie chickens are **endangered** and near **extinction.** This species of prairie chickens once numbered in the millions. Their **habitat** disappeared with the spread of cities, however, and grazing cattle took over pastures where they lived. Attwater Prairie Chicken National Wildlife Refuge is a tallgrass prairie near Eagle Lake. It provides a safe place for prairie chickens to nest.

To attract females, the male struts, spreads its feathers, and stomps its feet. It makes a noise called "booming" by letting air out of the orange-yellow sac under its neck. Although the males will perform their courtship dance on any flat surface, the birds nest only in a tallgrass prairie.

A male Attwater's prairie chicken is best recognized by the orange sac under its neck.

In June 2002, Kemp's Ridley sea turtle females laid their eggs on the only part of Galveston Island where cars are allowed to park on the beach. Since the turtles are endangered, they were given higher priority than the cars.

Kemp's Ridley Sea Turtle

Kemp's Ridley turtles, like other sea turtles, lay their eggs on the beach. **Hatchlings** race for the water to escape gulls and other **predators.** Only a few will survive to adulthood in the ocean. Of those that do survive, females return 15 to 40 years later to the same beach where they were hatched and lay their eggs there. In the 1960s, people were eating so many of the Kemp's Ridley eggs that this sea turtle was near extinction.

The major nesting place for Kemp's Ridley sea turtles is in Mexico, south of Brownsville. A group of **conservationists** gathered eggs from those nests. They brought the eggs to South Padre Island to hatch and release. They were successful in getting the turtles to return and establish a population again in Texas.

Old Rip, Texas Horned Lizard

The Texas horned lizard, which is the state reptile, is often called the horned toad. This **threatened** animal eats insects and can squirt blood from its eyes. One horned toad, Old Rip, is a legend. Eastland County built a new courthouse about 100 years ago. Officials marked the event by putting official papers inside a cornerstone and sealing it shut. Thirty years later, they opened the cornerstone and found a live horned toad. They named him Old Rip, after Rip Van Winkle, a fictional character who slept for twenty years.

Endangered Cats

Endangered ocelots and jaguarundi are found in the Santa Ana National Wildlife Refuge. They are also found in Lower Rio Grande Valley NWR, along with endangered bobcats and mountain lions.

Ocelots once lived throughout southern Texas. Today, fewer than 100 of them live in the state.

The hedgehog cactus blooms in Big Bend National Park.

Endangered and Threatened Plants

Many plant **species** in Texas today are endangered or threatened. One endangered plant is the Texas wild-rice. The headwaters of the San Marcos River is the only place where this plant grows. The plant's three-foot-long leaves and ten-foot-long stems stay completely underwater, except when flowers briefly come to the surface. Human activity on the river, such as boating and tubing, has caused the number of Texas wild-rice plants to decrease.

The Texas poppy-mallow is another endangered plant. Much of its **habitat** along the Colorado River has been lost to farming and development. The Chisos Mountains hedgehog cactus is another of the plants that are threatened in the state.

Some Species in Danger in Texas

Endangered

Amphibians
Houston toad
Texas blind salamander

Birds
Attwater's prairie chicken
black-capped vireo
golden-cheeked warbler
ivory-billed woodpecker
red-cockaded woodpecker
whooping crane

Fish
Comanche Springs pupfish
fountain darter
Pecos gambusia
Rio Grande silvery minnow

Mammals
blue whale
grater long-nosed bat
gray wolf
jaguar
ocelot
West Indian manatee

Reptiles
Kemp's Ridley sea turtle
leatherback sea turtle

Plants
black lace cactus
large-fruited sand-verbena
South Texas ambrosia
star cactus
Texas poppy-mallow
Texas prairie dawn
Texas snowbells
Texas wild-rice

Threatened

Amphibians
black-spotted newt
comal blind salamander
Mexican tree frog
San Marcos salamander

Birds
bald eagle
cactus gerruginous pygmy owl
Mexican spotted owl
reddish egret
sooty tern
white-faced ibis
wood stork

Fish
Mexican stoneroller
Rio Grande darter
River goby
Shovelnose sturgeon

Mammals
Atlantic spotted dolphin
black bear
margay
spotted bat
Texas kangaroo rat

Reptiles
alligator snapping turtle
green sea turtle
loggerhead sea turtle
reticulated gecko
scarlet snake
speckled racer
Texas horned lizard
timber (canebrake) rattlesnake

Plants
Chisos Mountains hedgehog cactus
Hinckley's oak
puzzle sunflower

Protecting Plants and Animals

Parks and zoos provide opportunities to see **native** plants and animals as well as ones not from Texas. The Texas State Aquarium, in Corpus Christi, built to resemble an underwater offshore drilling rig, allows visitors to view marine plants and animals at different depths.

Fossil Rim Wildlife Center, in Glen Rose, has some of the most **endangered** animals in the world, including white rhinos, cheetahs, and African oryxes. Animals run free on 1,500 acres of land. It also has a specific program to raise Attwater's prairie chickens.

The Gladys Porter Zoo, in Brownsville, was a gift from Gladys Sams Porter. It exhibits animals in natural **habitats** and is noted for its work to save endangered wildlife. Gladys Porter Zoo has over 1,500 animals from Asia,

Maned wolves make their home in the Fossil Rim Wildlife Center.

Africa, Australia, and tropical South America. The Fort Worth Zoo was the first in the nation to create a rain forest. The Houston Museum of Natural History has a collection of different kinds of butterflies, and visitors can walk through a live collection of butterflies.

Exotic Animals

Texas has the largest collection of **exotic** animals in the United States. Many of the animals are in **captivity** for their protection from people and other **predators.** The YO Ranch, near Kerrville is a 120-year-old working ranch. It has 50 exotic animal species, the largest collection in North America.

The Texas Snow Monkey **Sanctuary** near Dilley, in Frio County, started with 350 macaques, or Japanese snow monkeys. The monkeys were going to be killed because they were damaging crops and stealing food in Japan. The snow monkeys at the sanctuary live longer and grow bigger than their relatives in Japan. Baboons no longer needed for research now come to live at the sanctuary as well.

Author and animal **activist** Cleveland Amory opened Black Beauty Ranch, west of Tyler, in 1970 to care

Bison roam the 1,000-acre Black Beauty Ranch.

for injured or unwanted animals. The elephants, bison, bobcats, and coyotes there were once used for research or entertainment. Burros used in Grand Canyon tours retire to Black Beauty Ranch. Nim, a chimpanzee who learned sign language, lived the last eighteen years of his life at the sanctuary.

In 1970, fountain darters were added to the list of endangered species. Protecting Texas's rivers and lakes helps protect the animals that live in them.

Protected Waters

Barton Springs pool is fed by the Edwards **Aquifer.** The pool is 900 feet long. The water stays a constant 68° Fahrenheit. The **endangered** Barton Springs salamander and the Texas blind salamander live at Barton Springs. Austin's rapid growth has caused concern that the Edwards Aquifer might dry up. To prevent this, the city has set aside areas where no buildings can be constructed.

Balmorhea State Recreation Area has a swimming pool nearly as big as two football fields. It gets its water from San Solomon Springs. The desert **wetland** formed by the flow is a protected **habitat** for **endangered** Comanche Springs pupfish and the Pecos gambusia.

Treaty Oak

Near downtown Austin, a lone live oak tree is all that remains of a grove known as the Council Oaks. Native Americans had meetings there. Tradition says that Stephen Austin and Comanche chiefs came here and worked out peaceful boundaries for the new Texas colony. When Sam Houston stopped at the Treaty Oak on the day he left Austin in 1861, he walked around the huge tree and told his servant the tree's history. In 1927, the American Forestry Service declared Austin's Treaty Oak to be the most perfect example of a North American tree. Then, in 1989, a man poisoned the 500-year-old tree and was sent to jail for his crime. In an effort to save the Treaty Oak, all the soil around the tree was replaced. Still, more than half the tree died. A cutting from the tree was planted so that part of the tree would remain if the rest died. Instead of dying, the tree is now producing acorns, and the cutting is also thriving.

Texas is a very large state, so there should be room for all of its **species** to live side-by-side. In reality, though, it takes the efforts of all Texans to maintain the state's natural balance. Areas of land have been set aside to help bring back species whose populations have become dangerously low. With continuing efforts from the people of Texas to protect wildlife, the state's wonderful variety of plants and animals will continue to thrive long into the future.

Map of Texas

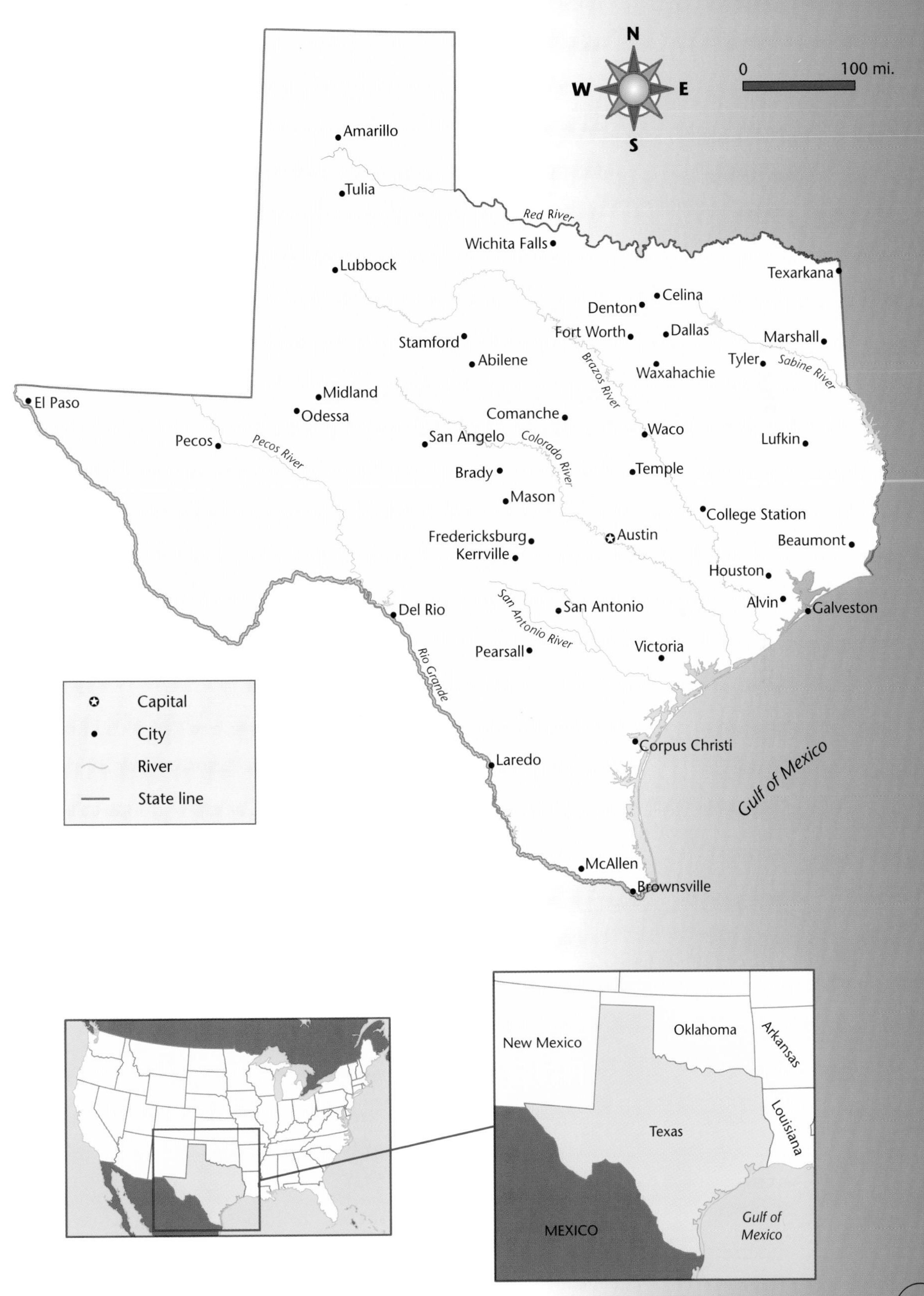

N
W
E
S
0
100 mi.
Amarillo
Tulia
Red River
Wichita Falls
Lubbock
Texarkana
Celina
Denton
Fort Worth
Dallas
Marshall
Stamford
Abilene
Tyler
Sabine River
Waxahachie
Brazos River
Midland
El Paso
Odessa
Comanche
Waco
Lufkin
Pecos
Pecos River
San Angelo
Colorado River
Brady
Temple
Mason
College Station
Fredericksburg
Kerrville
Austin
Beaumont
Houston
Alvin
Galveston
Del Rio
San Antonio River
San Antonio
Pearsall
Victoria
Rio Grande
Capital
City
River
State line
Corpus Christi
Laredo
Gulf of Mexico
McAllen
Brownsville
New Mexico
Oklahoma
Arkansas
Louisiana
Texas
MEXICO
Gulf of Mexico

Glossary

activist someone who actively supports a position or tries to help a cause

altitude height above a certain level, usually sea level

aquifer underground place that contains water that can be reached by wells

bivalve marine animal that has two hinged shells

bottomland soil along the banks of a river

brush heavy growth of bushes and small trees

captivity under control of humans, often in a zoo

climate weather conditions that are usual for a certain area

concentration amount of something in a certain area

conservationist someone who assists with preservation and protection of natural resources

descend to be born of; to come from a given source

ecosystem community of living things, together with the environment in which they live

elevation height above sea level

endangered at risk of dying out

era important period in time

eroding wearing away by wind or water

exotic brought to one area from another

extinct no longer living

extirpated no longer living within a certain area

food chain diagram of the plants and animals that need one another for food within a single habitat

food web several food chains combined within an ecosystem

fossils remains of animals or plants that have turned to stone

geological relating to the study of rocks and the history of Earth

glacier very large sheet of ice that spreads very slowly over land

habitat place where an animal or plant lives and grows

hatchling animal recently hatched from an egg

ice age period of time when temperatures were lower and a large part of Earth was covered with ice

longitude distance measured in degrees east or west of an imaginary line drawn between the North and South poles

mammal warm-blooded animal with a backbone; female mammals produce milk to feed their young

marsh wet, low-lying area, often thick with tall grasses

meridian imaginary line running north and south on a map

migrate move from one place to another for food or to breed

mollusk sea creature with a soft body protected by a hard shell

native originally from a certain area

playa round, sunken place that fills with water when it rains

predator animal that lives mostly by killing and eating other animals

prehistoric from the time before history was written

refuge safe place

reintroduce bring back to an area

reservation place that is set aside for a certain purpose

sanctuary place of safety

savanna grassy plain with few trees

semi-desert having desertlike qualities, but with more annual rainfall

species group of plants or animals that look and behave the same way

supercontinent former large continent that broke apart to form all the current continents

territory land on which an animal or animals live and that an animal will defend

thicket tangled forest of vines and trees

threatened group of animals whose numbers are decreasing, bringing the group close to endangerment

urban relating to the city

watershed area that drains into a body of water

wetland very wet, low-lying land

xeriscape shrubs and grasses that require very little water

More Books to Read

Campbell, Linda. *Endangered and Threatened Animals of Texas.* Austin, Tex.: Texas Parks and Wildlife Department, 1996.

Lockwood, Mark W. *Learn About Texas Birds.* Austin, Tex.: Texas Parks and Wildlife Department, 1997.

Zappler, Georg. *Learn About Texas Fish.* Austin, Tex.: Texas Parks and Wildlife Department, 2001.

Zappler, Georg. *Learn about Texas Insects.* Austin, Tex.: Texas Parks and Wildlife Department, 1999.

Index

About the Author

Mary Dodson Wade spent 25 years as an elementary school librarian. Now she writes full time and has more than 40 books in print, with more to come. She lives in Houston, Texas, and loves to write about her favorite state. Mary also has traveled the world with her husband.